INVENTIONS AND DISCOVERY

THE WRIGHT BROTHERS AND THE AIRPLANE

by Xavier Niz

illustrated by Steve Erwin,

Keith Williams, and

Charles Barnett III

Consultant:
Darrell Collins, Historian
Wright Brothers National Memorial
Manteo, North Carolina

Capstone
press®

Mankato, Minnesota

Graphic Library is published by Capstone Press,
1710 Roe Crest Drive, North Mankato, Minnesota 56003.
www.capstonepress.com

Library of Congress Cataloging-in-Publication Data
Niz, Xavier.
    The Wright brothers and the airplane / by Xavier Niz; illustrated by Steve Erwin, Keith
Williams, and Charles Barnett III.
    p. cm. —(Graphic library—inventions and discovery)
    Summary: "In graphic novel format, tells the story of how Wilbur and Orville Wright
developed, tested, and successfully flew the first powered airplane"—Provided by publisher.
    Includes bibliographical references and index.
    ISBN-13: 978-0-7368-6845-7 (hardcover)
    ISBN-10: 0-7368-6845-3 (hardcover)
    ISBN-13: 978-0-7368-7897-5 (softcover pbk.)
    ISBN-10: 0-7368-7897-1 (softcover pbk.)
    1. Wright, Orville, 1871–1948—Juvenile literature. 2. Wright, Wilbur, 1867–1912—
Juvenile literature. 3. Aeronautics—United States—Biography—Juvenile literature. I. Erwin,
Steve, ill. II. Williams, Keith, 1958 Feb. 24– III. Barnett, Charles, III, ill. IV. Title. V. Series.
TL540.W7N59 2007
629.130092'273—dc22
[B]   2006023376

Designers
Bob Lentz and Thomas Emery

Colorist
Melissa Kaercher

Editor
Christine Peterson

Editor's note: Direct quotations from primary sources are indicated by a yellow background.

Direct quotations appear on the following pages:
Page 10, quote by Wilbur Wright as published in *The Bishop's Boys: A Life of Wilbur and
    Orville Wright* by Tom D. Crouch (New York: W. W. Norton, 1989).
Page 13, quote by Wilbur Wright as documented in *The Wright Brothers: A Biography
    Authorized by Orville Wright* by Fred C. Kelly (New York: Harcourt, Brace, and
    Company, 1943).

Printed in the United States   5960

TABLE OF CONTENTS

CHAPTER 1

THE DREAM OF FLIGHT

Wilbur and his younger brother Orville were two of Milton and Susan Wright's many children. The family lived in Dayton, Ohio, in the late 1800s. Milton and Susan encouraged their children to ask questions and explore the world around them.

It says here that Alexander Graham Bell has figured out how to send sound across wires. How does that work, Father?

I'm not sure, Wilbur. What do you think, Orville?

I'll bet it has something to do with electricity.

In 1896, Orville became ill. Wilbur read to him each night while he recovered. At that time, early aviators were making news.

Remember Lilienthal, Orville? It says here that he died when a wind gust caught his glider, and it crashed.

Sounds like he had no way to control it.

Reading about Lilienthal and problems with flight sparked an interest in the Wright brothers. They read many books about early experimenters in flight. Wilbur and Orville soon discovered all these pioneers faced a similar problem.

American engineer Octave Chanute has built several successful gliders.

Yes, but he still can't control the machine in flight.

The Wright brothers set out to solve the problem of controlled flight. They began by studying birds.

That bird turned left by changing the angle of its wings.

How can we make a glider do the same thing?

7

We'll need more lift for powered flight.

Perhaps there's something wrong with Lilienthal's data?

I'm beginning to think that not within a thousand years would man ever fly!

After returning to Dayton, Orville and Wilbur built a wind tunnel to test different wing designs. They tested at least 200 types of wing surfaces, curves, and angles.

After we test these wings, we'll have enough data for our own air pressure tables.

That new wing shape should create more lift. A rear rudder would also make the glider more stable.

The Wright brothers returned to Kitty Hawk in September 1902 to test their new designs. After several successful glider flights, Wilbur and Orville were ready for a new challenge.

I think we are ready to build a powered machine.

13

The Wrights returned to Kitty Hawk in September 1903, determined to prove their designs would work. But engine problems sent Orville back to Dayton for repairs. Finally, on December 14, their new powered flying machine, called the Flyer, was ready for its first test.

You won the coin toss, Wilbur, so you get to pilot the Flyer.

Don't look so glum, Orville. You'll get your chance.

Seconds later the powered machine crashed into the sand.

Are you all right?

I'm fine. Let's get the Flyer back to the shop.

I hope the wind dies down.

We'll need to test the Flyer again soon. Winter is coming.

On December 17, 1903, Orville and Wilbur decided to try one last flight. By 10:30 that morning, the Wrights and their crew had the Flyer positioned on its wooden launching rail.

Orville successfully flew for 12 seconds and covered 120 feet. The brothers made three other flights that day. The longest flight lasted 59 seconds and covered 852 feet. Together, Orville and Wilbur became the first people in history to fly a heavier-than-air, controlled, powered aircraft.

With a few changes, the Wrights' new Flyer III could fly for several miles, make sharp turns, and land under its own power. In 1905, the Wright brothers decided to sell their new design to U.S. Signal Corps.

Signal Corps leaders heard our Flyer doesn't work. They want to see a demonstration.

Our lawyer told us not to demonstrate our designs until we have the patents to protect them.

Finally, on May 23, 1906, the Wrights received their patents.

In the years that followed the Wrights' success at Kitty Hawk, aviators in other countries continued developing powered flight. In November 1906, a Brazilian pilot named Alberto Santos-Dumont made several public flights in France.

Reporters make it sound like Santos-Dumont was the first to pilot a powered flying machine.

Let's see those Americans top this.

If the Wrights' airplanes can even fly at all.

But he only traveled 425 feet in his machine. One of us should show the French what a Wright flyer can do.

CHAPTER 4

AVIATION TAKES OFF

In 1909, Wilbur and Orville formed the Wright Company to sell their airplanes. They continued to design new aircraft. In 1910, they introduced the Wright Model B.

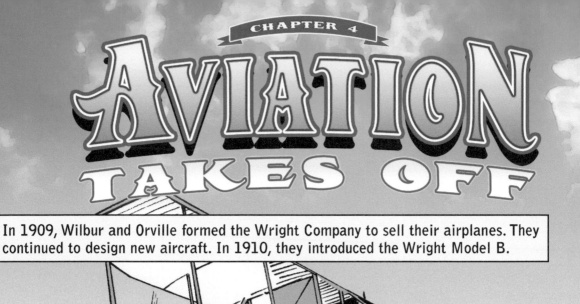

This model is our best yet.

Adding wheels to the skids was a great idea, Orville.

The Wrights' aircraft continued to set records. On September 17, 1911, Calbraith Rodgers set out to make the first airplane flight across the United States. He left New York in a Wright airplane nicknamed the *Vin Fiz* after a popular soda.

The trip should be smooth going in this Wright EX.

I'll be following you by train. Just set the plane down if you have any problems.

Rodger's trip was anything but smooth. The *Vin Fiz* crashed several times. Charlie Taylor repaired or replaced parts wherever the plane went down.

On December 10, Rodgers finally arrived in Long Beach, California.

There's the Vin Fiz!

Amazing!

25

For the next few years, Orville and Wilbur continued to improve their airplanes. Although the brothers tried new designs, their control system remained basically unchanged from that first powered flight at Kitty Hawk.

Unfortunately, tragedy was waiting around the corner. On May 30, 1912, Wilbur died from typhoid fever.

Orville took over the business after Wilbur died. Tired of running the company alone, he sold the business in 1915. Orville retired to his laboratory where he invented the first autopilot, a robot biplane, and a successful toy called Flips and Flops.

On January 30, 1948, Orville Wright died.

Today, airplanes carry people, food, and packages almost anywhere on earth.

Military aircraft can strike anywhere in the world.

Aviators and scientists continue the Wright brothers' work. Only 66 years after the first flight at Kitty Hawk, flight made history again with the *Apollo 11* moon landing.

Today, space shuttles use movable edges on their wings to control roll. These ailerons follow the same idea as the Wright brothers' wing warping.

NASA

United States

USA

MORE ABOUT THE WRIGHT BROTHERS AND THE AIRPLANE

- Wilbur Wright was born April 16, 1867, near Millville, Indiana. He died May 30, 1912, in Dayton, Ohio.

- Orville Wright was born August 19, 1871, in Dayton, Ohio. He died January 30, 1948, after suffering a heart attack in his laboratory in Dayton.

- One of the earliest inventors to study flight was Leonardo Da Vinci. In 1490, he made several attempts to design a flying machine, including a screwlike propeller that was an early model of the helicopter.

- During their trips to Kitty Hawk, the brothers struggled with the wind, cold, sand, and bugs that swept across the dunes. At first, they camped in a small tent. Later, Orville and Wilbur built a small shed where they lived, and a hangar for their gliders and the Flyer.

- Members of the U.S. Lifesaving Station at Kill Devil Hills helped the Wright brothers with takeoffs and landings. When Orville and Wilbur were ready to test their gliders and Flyers, they tacked a red flag to the side of the hangar. When crew members saw the flag, they headed to the dunes to help with the aircraft.

The Wright brothers flew their 1902 glider at least 1,000 times off the sand dunes at Kitty Hawk. This glider set all the world records for gliding at that time, including one glide that went 622.5 feet in just 21 seconds. After the success of their 1902 glider, the Wright brothers were ready to build their powered machine.

Some aviators claimed that they, not the Wright brothers, invented the airplane. In 1914, aircraft manufacturer Glenn Curtiss rebuilt and flew a version of the Great Aerodrome. This aircraft was invented by Samuel Langley in 1903. Langley had little success flying the large craft. Curtiss was able to fly the Aerodrome only after making several changes to Langley's design. Despite the changes, officials at the Smithsonian Institution declared that Langley invented the airplane. Orville fought this claim until 1942, when Smithsonian officials admitted that the Wright brothers were the airplane's true inventors. Today, millions of people view the first Wright Flyer at the Smithsonian.

When *Apollo 11* astronaut Neil Armstrong walked on the moon, he paid tribute to the Wright brothers. In Armstrong's pocket was a piece of fabric from the Wright brothers' 1903 Flyer.

GLOSSARY

bank (BANGK)—to tilt an airplane sideways when turning

horsepower (HORSS-pou-ur)—a unit for measuring an engine's power

lift (LIFT)—the force that lets an airplane rise from the ground and stay in the air

patent (PAT-uhnt)—a legal document that gives an inventor the right to make, use, or sell an invention for a set period of years

pitch (PICH)—the angle of the blades on an aircraft; pitch determines whether an aircraft moves up or down.

roll (ROHL)—the movement of an airplane from side to side

skeptical (SKEP-tuh-kuhl)—to doubt that something is true

yaw (YAW)—the movement of an aircraft's nose from side to side

INTERNET SITES

FactHound offers a safe, fun way to find Internet sites related to this book. All of the sites on FactHound have been researched by our staff.

Here's how:
1. Visit *www.facthound.com*
2. Choose your grade level.
3. Type in this book ID **0736868453** for age-appropriate sites. You may also browse subjects by clicking on letters, or by clicking on pictures and words.
4. Click on the **Fetch It** button.

FactHound will fetch the best sites for you!

READ MORE

Hill, Lee Sullivan. *The Flyer Flew!: The Invention of the Airplane.* On My Own Science. Minneapolis: Millbrook Press, 2006.

Lynch, Emma. *The Wright Brothers.* Lives and Times. Chicago: Heinemann, 2005.

Masters, Nancy Robinson. *The Airplane.* Inventions that Shaped the World. New York: Franklin Watts, 2004.

Orr, Tamra. *The Dawn of Aviation: The Story of the Wright Brothers.* Monumental Milestones. Hockessin, Del.: Mitchell Lane, 2005.

BIBLIOGRAPHY

Crouch, Tom D. *The Bishop's Boys: A Life of Wilbur and Orville Wright.* New York: W. W. Norton, 1989.

Kelly, Fred C. *The Wright Brothers: A Biography Authorized by Orville Wright.* New York: Harcourt, Brace, and Company, 1943.

National Park Service: The Wright Brothers National Memorial (http://www.nps.gov/wrbr/).

Wright, Orville. *How We Invented the Airplane: An Illustrated History.* New York: Dover, 1988.

INDEX